BUILD YOUR BUSINESS PLANNER

ONE DAY AT A TIME

TONI B B

BOSS UP

8 Tips on How to Start a Business

Every day, a new business emerges, and another one dies or remains stagnant, yet so many other businesses keep growing and maximizing profits day by day. Starting a business is not as simple as it seems, it requires a lot of motivation, hard work, and a dogged focus to keep moving on no matter what. If you say starting a business is very easy and is 100 percent stress-free; then, I will tell you that failing in business is the easiest thing to do too. The point is not about how easy or hard, or tough or stressful it is to get started – take your mind off that. You should rather focus your attention on starting the business and keeping it running successfully no matter what. I will present successful tips to help you start your business, the type that will succeed always. Below are the 8 tips on how to start a business.

1. Be Determined

You have to be doggedly determined about what you want to do. You have to be set and ready to put in all that is required to see the business gets started and succeed as well. Make sure you are strong and focused enough to withstand tough business times when they come, because they will surely come. At this point, you have to build yourself from within with the right qualities that will help you survive and eventually succeed. So, get the right amount of zeal, focus, resistance, patience, persistence and determination injected into your system to self-start your company. The first step is to build your inward person with all the strength and skills required, before building the business.

2. Create You Finished Product or Service

A business is all about bringing solution to people with a particular product or service you offer. It is not just about your idea. No matter how good your idea is, if it does not become a finished product or service that someone can use and relate with it remains useless in the market. So, it time to go to the drawing board and transform that wonderful idea to a tangible service that benefits its target. It could be a piece of software; it could be a training service, or whatever. Just make sure it has been packaged ready to be delivered to clients. Set it up and be ready to go with it.

3. Create your Business Plan

A good business plan is what keeps you focused and organized. This is the blueprint of your business for intending partners and inventors to see and quickly understand what the business is about. To begin, write out the business vision or mission, write a summary line, and enumerate your services as well. Take time out to draw out a perfect business plan. You can get a business plan template online to use as a way of simplifying the process.

4. Register your Business and Get a Website

Make your business a recognized entity by registering the business name with the government agency. With this name you will create business bank accounts and build a brand that people will identify with. Also register a domain name for your business, design and host a website to establish your business presence online for all to have access to it.

5. Identify your Target Market

To succeed in your business, you have to know from the beginning those that your product or service are meant for. It cannot be for everyone. This will help you narrow down your efforts to focus on those that are willing to buy from you right from the start. It will help your business a lot if you immediately know who to focus your marketing efforts on. You are aware of the exact type of clients to approach with your services and products. This will produce better output.

6. Calculate Cost of Production and Product Price

You will need to find out and calculate the total amount of money spent in the production of your product from the initial stage until it is ready to be bought and delivered. If it is a service, then evaluate the cost of creating and presenting that service to the target users. After calculating the cost of Production, then fix a price for your product or service that is above the cost of production to maintain a profit margin.

7. Start Production and Service on a Small Scale

It is a good idea to begin production on a small scale, even if you have all the money to make it as big as possible. The first stages of production and service rendering might not receive much patronage, so it is wise to keep it very simple. This will help you save cost and minimize lost as much as possible. Just imagine if your new business was a bakery, and you started off producing so much bread, if they are not all sold, the product will be spoilt, making you to incur losses at the beginning.

8. Use Social Media to Promote Your Brand

Use the popular social media networks and other marketing strategies to spread the word about your new business. Continue on these platforms to build and maintain a strong and loyal customer base.

Yearly Overview

	VIEWS	VISITS	SALES	REVENUE	FEES
JAN					
FEB					
MAR					
APR					
MAY					
JUN					
JUL					
AUG					
SEP					
OKT					
NOV					
DEC					

Business Overview

NAME

PHONE

GOAL

EMAIL

MANTRA

BUSINESS ADDRESS

ABOUT

COMPETITION

TARGET AUDIENCE

GENDER

INTERESTS

AGE RANGE

LOCATION

PROFESSION

INCOME

LIVING PLACE

Yearly Goals

GOAL

WHY
_____
_____
_____
_____
_____
_____
_____

START DATE   DUE DATE

GOAL

WHY
_____
_____
_____
_____
_____
_____
_____
_____

START DATE   DUE DATE

GOAL

WHY
_____
_____
_____
_____
_____
_____
_____

START DATE   DUE DATE

Monthly Calendar

MONTH/YEAR:

Sunday	Monday	Tuesday	Wednesday	Thursday	Friday	Saturday

NOTES

Business Goals Monthly

Month

Goals	Action Steps
Events	
Ideas	
Sales	

This monthly goals by weeks

DATE:

WEEK 1

_____
_____
_____
_____

WEEK 2

_____
_____
_____
_____

WEEK 3

_____
_____
_____
_____

WEEK 4

_____
_____
_____
_____

GOALS

MAKE IT HAPPEN

_____
_____
_____
_____

Weekly Planner

DATE:

MON

TUE

WED

THU

FRI

SAT

SUN

PRIORITIES

TO DO

_____
_____
_____
_____
_____
_____
_____

NOTES

Weekly Planner

DATE:

MON

TUE

WED

THU

FRI

SAT

SUN

PRIORITIES

TO DO

_____
_____
_____
_____
_____
_____
_____
_____

NOTES

Weekly Planner

DATE:

MON

TUE

WED

THU

FRI

SAT

SUN

PRIORITIES

TO DO

_____
_____
_____
_____
_____
_____
_____
_____

NOTES

Weekly Planner

DATE:

MON

TUE

WED

THU

FRI

SAT

SUN

PRIORITIES

TO DO

_____

_____

_____

_____

_____

_____

_____

_____

NOTES

Monthly Calendar

MONTH/YEAR:

Sunday	Monday	Tuesday	Wednesday	Thursday	Friday	Saturday

NOTES

Business Goals Monthly

Month

Goals	Action Steps
Events	
Ideas	
Sales	

This monthly goals by weeks

DATE:

WEEK 1

_____
_____
_____
_____

WEEK 2

_____
_____
_____
_____

WEEK 3

_____
_____
_____
_____

WEEK 4

_____
_____
_____
_____

GOALS

MAKE IT HAPPEN

_____
_____
_____
_____

Weekly Planner

DATE:

MON	
TUE	
WED	
THU	
FRI	
SAT	
SUN	

PRIORITIES

TO DO

_____

_____

_____

_____

_____

_____

_____

NOTES

Weekly Planner

DATE:

MON

TUE

WED

THU

FRI

SAT

SUN

PRIORITIES

TO DO

_____
_____
_____
_____
_____
_____
_____
_____

NOTES

Weekly Planner

DATE:

MON

TUE

WED

THU

FRI

SAT

SUN

PRIORITIES

TO DO

_____

_____

_____

_____

_____

_____

_____

NOTES

Weekly Planner

DATE:

MON

TUE

WED

THU

FRI

SAT

SUN

PRIORITIES

TO DO

_____
_____
_____
_____
_____
_____
_____

NOTES

Monthly Calendar

MONTH/YEAR:

Sunday	Monday	Tuesday	Wednesday	Thursday	Friday	Saturday

NOTES

Business Goals Monthly

Month

Goals	Action Steps
Events	
Ideas	
Sales	

This monthly goals by weeks

DATE:

WEEK 1

_____
_____
_____

_____

WEEK 2

_____
_____
_____

_____

WEEK 3

_____
_____
_____

_____

WEEK 4

_____
_____
_____

_____

GOALS

MAKE IT HAPPEN

_____

_____

_____

_____

Weekly Planner

DATE:

MON

TUE

WED

THU

FRI

SAT

SUN

PRIORITIES

TO DO

_____

_____

_____

_____

_____

_____

_____

_____

NOTES

Weekly Planner

DATE:

MON

TUE

WED

THU

FRI

SAT

SUN

PRIORITIES

TO DO

_____

_____

_____

_____

_____

_____

_____

_____

NOTES

Weekly Planner

DATE:

MON

TUE

WED

THU

FRI

SAT

SUN

PRIORITIES

TO DO

_____

_____

_____

_____

_____

_____

_____

_____

NOTES

Weekly Planner

DATE:

MON

TUE

WED

THU

FRI

SAT

SUN

PRIORITIES

TO DO

_____
_____
_____
_____
_____
_____
_____
_____

NOTES

"You're most unhappy customers are your greatest source of learning"

Monthly Calendar

MONTH/YEAR:

Sunday	Monday	Tuesday	Wednesday	Thursday	Friday	Saturday

NOTES

Business Goals Monthly

Month

Goals	Action Steps
Goals	
Events	
Ideas	
Sales	

This monthly goals by weeks

DATE:

WEEK 1

_____
_____
_____
_____

WEEK 2

_____
_____
_____
_____

WEEK 3

_____
_____
_____
_____

WEEK 4

_____
_____
_____
_____

GOALS

MAKE IT HAPPEN

_____
_____
_____
_____

Weekly Planner

DATE:

MON

TUE

WED

THU

FRI

SAT

SUN

PRIORITIES

TO DO

_____

_____

_____

_____

_____

_____

_____

_____

NOTES

Weekly Planner

DATE:

MON

TUE

WED

THU

FRI

SAT

SUN

PRIORITIES

TO DO

_____

_____

_____

_____

_____

_____

_____

_____

NOTES

Weekly Planner

DATE:

MON

TUE

WED

THU

FRI

SAT

SUN

PRIORITIES

TO DO

_____
_____
_____
_____
_____
_____
_____
_____

NOTES

Weekly Planner

DATE:

MON

TUE

WED

THU

FRI

SAT

SUN

PRIORITIES

TO DO

_____
_____
_____
_____
_____
_____
_____
_____

NOTES

Monthly Calendar

MONTH/YEAR:

Sunday	Monday	Tuesday	Wednesday	Thursday	Friday	Saturday

NOTES

Business Goals Monthly

Month

Goals	Action Steps
Events	
Ideas	
Sales	

This monthly goals by weeks

DATE:

WEEK 1   GOALS

_____   ....
_____   .   .
_____   .   .
_____   .   .
                                    ....

WEEK 2

_____   ....
_____   .   .
_____   .   .
_____   .   .
                                    ....

WEEK 3

_____   ....
_____   .   .
_____   .   .
_____   .   .
                                    ....

WEEK 4

_____   ....
_____   .   .
_____   .   .
_____   .   .
                                    ....

MAKE IT HAPPEN

_____
_____
_____
_____

Weekly Planner

DATE:

MON

TUE

WED

THU

FRI

SAT

SUN

PRIORITIES

TO DO

_____
_____
_____
_____
_____
_____
_____
_____

NOTES

Weekly Planner

DATE:

MON

TUE

WED

THU

FRI

SAT

SUN

PRIORITIES

TO DO

_____

_____

_____

_____

_____

_____

_____

_____

NOTES

Weekly Planner

DATE:

MON

TUE

WED

THU

FRI

SAT

SUN

PRIORITIES

TO DO

_____
_____
_____
_____
_____
_____
_____
_____

NOTES

Weekly Planner

DATE:

MON

TUE

WED

THU

FRI

SAT

SUN

PRIORITIES

TO DO

_____

_____

_____

_____

_____

_____

_____

NOTES

Monthly Calendar

MONTH/YEAR:

Sunday	Monday	Tuesday	Wednesday	Thursday	Friday	Saturday

NOTES

Business Goals Monthly

Month

Goals

Events

Ideas

Sales

Action Steps

This monthly goals by weeks

DATE:

WEEK 1

_____
_____
_____
_____

WEEK 2

_____
_____
_____
_____

WEEK 3

_____
_____
_____
_____

WEEK 4

_____
_____
_____
_____

GOALS

MAKE IT HAPPEN

_____
_____
_____
_____

Weekly Planner

DATE:

MON

TUE

WED

THU

FRI

SAT

SUN

PRIORITIES

TO DO

_____
_____
_____
_____
_____
_____
_____
_____

NOTES

Weekly Planner

DATE:

MON

TUE

WED

THU

FRI

SAT

SUN

PRIORITIES

TO DO

_____
_____
_____
_____
_____
_____
_____

NOTES

Weekly Planner

DATE:

MON	PRIORITIES
TUE	
WED	TO DO
THU	_____
FRI	_____
SAT	NOTES
SUN	

Weekly Planner

DATE:

MON

TUE

WED

THU

FRI

SAT

SUN

PRIORITIES

TO DO

_____
_____
_____
_____
_____
_____
_____
_____

NOTES

Monthly Calendar

MONTH/YEAR:

Sunday	Monday	Tuesday	Wednesday	Thursday	Friday	Saturday

NOTES

Business Goals Monthly

Month

Goals	Action Steps

Goals

Events

Ideas

Sales

This monthly goals by weeks

DATE:

WEEK 1

_____
_____
_____
_____

WEEK 2

_____
_____
_____
_____

WEEK 3

_____
_____
_____
_____

WEEK 4

_____
_____
_____
_____

GOALS

MAKE IT HAPPEN

_____
_____
_____
_____

Weekly Planner

DATE:

MON

TUE

WED

THU

FRI

SAT

SUN

PRIORITIES

TO DO

_____
_____
_____
_____
_____
_____
_____
_____

NOTES

Weekly Planner

DATE:

MON

TUE

WED

THU

FRI

SAT

SUN

PRIORITIES

TO DO

_____
_____
_____
_____
_____
_____
_____

NOTES

Weekly Planner

DATE:

MON

TUE

WED

THU

FRI

SAT

SUN

PRIORITIES

TO DO

_____
_____
_____
_____
_____
_____
_____
_____

NOTES

Weekly Planner

DATE:

MON

TUE

WED

THU

FRI

SAT

SUN

PRIORITIES

TO DO

_____
_____
_____
_____
_____
_____
_____
_____

NOTES

Monthly Calendar

MONTH/YEAR:

Sunday	Monday	Tuesday	Wednesday	Thursday	Friday	Saturday

NOTES

Business Goals Monthly

Month

Goals

Events

Ideas

Sales

Action Steps

This monthly goals by weeks

DATE:

WEEK 1

_____
_____
_____
_____

WEEK 2

_____
_____
_____
_____

WEEK 3

_____
_____
_____
_____

WEEK 4

_____
_____
_____
_____

GOALS

MAKE IT HAPPEN

_____
_____
_____
_____

Weekly Planner

DATE:

MON

TUE

WED

THU

FRI

SAT

SUN

PRIORITIES

TO DO

_____
_____
_____
_____
_____
_____
_____
_____

NOTES

Weekly Planner

DATE:

MON

TUE

WED

THU

FRI

SAT

SUN

PRIORITIES

TO DO

_____
_____
_____
_____
_____
_____
_____
_____

NOTES

Weekly Planner

DATE:

MON

TUE

WED

THU

FRI

SAT

SUN

PRIORITIES

TO DO

_____

_____

_____

_____

_____

_____

_____

_____

NOTES

Weekly Planner

DATE:

MON

TUE

WED

THU

FRI

SAT

SUN

PRIORITIES

TO DO

_____

_____

_____

_____

_____

_____

_____

NOTES

Monthly Calendar

MONTH/YEAR:

Sunday	Monday	Tuesday	Wednesday	Thursday	Friday	Saturday

NOTES

Business Goals Monthly

Month

Goals

Events

Ideas

Sales

Action Steps

This monthly goals by weeks

DATE:

WEEK 1

_____
_____
_____
_____

WEEK 2

_____
_____
_____
_____

WEEK 3

_____
_____
_____
_____

WEEK 4

_____
_____
_____
_____

GOALS

MAKE IT HAPPEN

_____
_____
_____
_____

Weekly Planner

DATE:

MON

TUE

WED

THU

FRI

SAT

SUN

PRIORITIES

TO DO

_____

_____

_____

_____

_____

_____

_____

_____

NOTES

Weekly Planner

DATE:

MON

TUE

WED

THU

FRI

SAT

SUN

PRIORITIES

TO DO

_____
_____
_____
_____
_____
_____
_____
_____

NOTES

Weekly Planner

DATE:

MON	
TUE	
WED	
THU	
FRI	
SAT	
SUN	

PRIORITIES

TO DO

_____

_____

_____

_____

_____

_____

_____

_____

NOTES

Weekly Planner

DATE:

MON

TUE

WED

THU

FRI

SAT

SUN

PRIORITIES

TO DO

_____
_____
_____
_____
_____
_____
_____
_____

NOTES

Monthly Calendar

MONTH/YEAR:

Sunday	Monday	Tuesday	Wednesday	Thursday	Friday	Saturday

NOTES

Business Goals Monthly

Month

Goals	Action Steps
Goals	
Events	
Ideas	
Sales	

This monthly goals by weeks

DATE:

WEEK 1

_____
_____
_____
_____

WEEK 2

_____
_____
_____
_____

WEEK 3

_____
_____
_____
_____

WEEK 4

_____
_____
_____
_____

GOALS

MAKE IT HAPPEN

_____
_____
_____
_____

Weekly Planner

DATE:

MON

TUE

WED

THU

FRI

SAT

SUN

PRIORITIES

TO DO

_____
_____
_____
_____
_____
_____
_____
_____

NOTES

Weekly Planner

DATE:

MON

TUE

WED

THU

FRI

SAT

SUN

PRIORITIES

TO DO

_____
_____
_____
_____
_____
_____
_____
_____

NOTES

Weekly Planner

DATE:

MON

TUE

WED

THU

FRI

SAT

SUN

PRIORITIES

TO DO

_____
_____
_____
_____
_____
_____
_____

NOTES

Weekly Planner

DATE:

MON

TUE

WED

THU

FRI

SAT

SUN

PRIORITIES

TO DO

_____
_____
_____
_____
_____
_____
_____
_____

NOTES

"plan right making a living, don't let poor planning prevent you from making life."

Monthly Calendar

MONTH/YEAR:

Sunday	Monday	Tuesday	Wednesday	Thursday	Friday	Saturday

NOTES

Business Goals Monthly

Month

Goals	Action Steps
Events	
Ideas	
Sales	

This monthly goals by weeks

DATE:

WEEK 1

_____

_____

_____

_____

WEEK 2

_____

_____

_____

_____

WEEK 3

_____

_____

_____

_____

WEEK 4

_____

_____

_____

_____

MAKE IT HAPPEN

_____

_____

_____

_____

GOALS

Weekly Planner

DATE:

MON

TUE

WED

THU

FRI

SAT

SUN

PRIORITIES

TO DO

_____
_____
_____
_____
_____
_____
_____
_____

NOTES

Weekly Planner

DATE:

MON

TUE

WED

THU

FRI

SAT

SUN

PRIORITIES

TO DO

_____

_____

_____

_____

_____

_____

_____

_____

NOTES

Weekly Planner

DATE:

MON

TUE

WED

THU

FRI

SAT

SUN

PRIORITIES

TO DO

_____
_____
_____
_____
_____
_____
_____
_____

NOTES

Weekly Planner

DATE:

MON	PRIORITIES
TUE	
WED	TO DO
THU	_____
FRI	_____
SAT	NOTES
SUN	

Monthly Calendar

MONTH/YEAR:

Sunday	Monday	Tuesday	Wednesday	Thursday	Friday	Saturday

NOTES

Business Goals Monthly

Month

Goals

Events

Ideas

Sales

Action Steps

This monthly goals by weeks

DATE:

WEEK 1

_____
_____
_____
_____

WEEK 2

_____
_____
_____
_____

WEEK 3

_____
_____
_____
_____

WEEK 4

_____
_____
_____
_____

MAKE IT HAPPEN

_____
_____
_____
_____

GOALS

Weekly Planner

DATE:

MON

TUE

WED

THU

FRI

SAT

SUN

PRIORITIES

TO DO

_____
_____
_____
_____
_____
_____
_____
_____

NOTES

Weekly Planner

DATE:

MON

TUE

WED

THU

FRI

SAT

SUN

PRIORITIES

TO DO

_____
_____
_____
_____
_____
_____
_____
_____

NOTES

Weekly Planner

DATE:

MON

TUE

WED

THU

FRI

SAT

SUN

PRIORITIES

TO DO

_____

_____

_____

_____

_____

_____

_____

_____

NOTES

Weekly Planner

DATE:

MON

TUE

WED

THU

FRI

SAT

SUN

PRIORITIES

TO DO

_____
_____
_____
_____
_____
_____
_____
_____

NOTES

Dressing your company image

As a small business owner or a start up entrepreneur, you're driven to succeed in your business while facing many challenges along the way. You need to wear multiple hats and prioritize your spending as you are dealing with a limited budget.

Here are 5 Practical Branding steps needed to differentiate your company from the competition, position your business as a premium provider and instill trust and confidence in your clients.

1. Brand Essence

Think of your favorite brands. How do they make you feel? What do they represent to you? Do you have an emotional connection with them?

A brand is exactly two things: it's the promise your offering makes to people, and the clothes that promise is dressed in.

Branding is about what your customers feel with regards to services you provide or products that you sell. This includes their overall experience with your company from the very first contact to seeing your visual materials, using your product or service and staying in touch.

You can influence what your target audience feels by carefully distilling answers to some of the following questions and delivering on your Brand promise every time a customer interacts with your **company:**

- What does your business stand for?

- What are your company's essence, deep conviction, long terms goal?

- How unique are you from your competition?

- What is your target audience?

2. Business Name

Once you understand your business's brand essence, it is time to come up with a name. The name needs to be meaningful, unique, memorable, and easy to pronounce.

There are multiple brainstorming techniques you can use to come up with various words. Some could be metaphoric, based on company's place of origin, descriptive, others consisting of two words combined into one or completely new sound combinations.

Then compare your ideas and see **which name:**

- Sounds stronger

- Feels right

- Works internationally

- Has a strong emotional appeal

- Easy to read and pronounce

Other important considerations also include the chosen word URL availability as well as Trademark availability.

3. Logotype Design

The logotype is one of the most important steps in your business's visual identity. It's the face of your business and the main visual icon that signifies all of the business essences that you've discovered. Visual execution of a logotype design shouldn't be taken lightly and needs to be based on all of the discovered information about your brand, competitors, and the target audience.

Each industry has its own visual language, it is important for the designer you work**with to:**

- Explore the existing competitive landscape to make sure your logotype stands out

- Brainstorm and use free association as those are valuable techniques that help to arrive at the unique combinations

- Sketch multiple ideas to ensure that your logotype will go beyond the common ideas

- Skillfully design/draw the final logotypes

Final logotype selection should be based on how well the visual represents the brand essence. On a more practical note, you need to make sure that the logotype works well in smaller sizes as well as black and white for use in various applications.

4. Corporate Style

You did a great job on discovering your business's unique personality, came up with a wonderful name and gave it an essence-filled face... You now need to discover its aura, its style, and emotional/visual presence. This step is important as it works as a foundation for all of the visual materials to be based on.

Imagery

Your choice of imagery is important to consider when creating a style. Have you seen photos of people with fake smiles that just don't look genuine? Or, perhaps, you've encountered clip art imagery that just doesn't communicate professionalism?

Your choice of visual language should be true to what your brand stands for. It needs to communicate your values and your true convictions.

- Showcase real people with genuine emotions and a caring attitude

- Carefully choose royalty-free illustrations and photography on the basis of professionalism and genuineness of the imagery

Typography

Typography is another major component of the overall brand. Like brands, fonts have personalities - they could be serious, light-hearted, casual, and friendly. As with imagery, you need to practice caution when selecting fonts - some (Comic Sans) just don't communicate professionalism and others (Arial) just lack in personality.

Look through multiple font resources to **purchase:**

- Unique fonts that highlight your brand and have a great personality to them

- The fonts are inexpensive and worth every penny.

Color Palette

The last Corporate Style consideration is the Color. Colors don't just visually influence us, they make us feel and behave differently. Various colors are used in healing environments to help aid patient's recovery or for pain management. Colors are also known to induce appetite (orange), relax (green) or excite (red-orange).

- See which color combinations work best with your brand's essence:

- Choose a couple of primary colors that would be used as main identifiers for your brand

- Also, pick some secondary ones for the background elements

- Select accent colors that could be used in limited amounts to highlighting important elements

Once the overall style has been established, all of the findings should be entered into a Brand Guidelines document. It could be as basic or as elaborate as needed.

The basic ones usually contain the above mentioned Corporate style elements and help in the creation of consistent and professional looking visual materials.

5. Visual Materials

Depending on your Sales and Marketing strategy choose various venues of customer communications.

You need to consistently and creatively apply your established corporate **style to:**

- Social networks pages (Linked-in, FB, Twitter)

- Website +Online communications (depth of information and credibility)

- Stationery (business cards, letterhead, and envelopes)

- Print materials (brochures, handouts, ads)

- Presentations (PowerPoint)

- Business documents (Invoicing, Estimates, and Forms)

Following the above 5 steps will ensure that your business's true essence successfully shines forth. You will have done a great job by putting your minds, hearts, and souls together. You will have created a visual foundation for your business to succeed in differentiating your company from the competition, positioning your business as a premium provider and instilling trust and confidence in your clients.

Is your wardrobe is holding you back? Have you taken the time to develop a personal style - one that reflects you? **Here are some rules to dress for success for your business:**

- **Express your individuality.** Remember, you are your brand. By being true to yourself you will be authentic. If you are warm, open, accessible dressing like a femme fatale won't cut it. You'll look silly and people will notice the disconnect immediately.

- **Know what you are selling.** If you need to come across as knowledgeable, insightful and savvy, then dressing in a mini skirt, no stockings, and midriff will project the opposite message.

- **Pay attention to who's looking.** Who are you trying to influence or persuade? What rules do they go by? Wear a pair of two-inch heels, freshly pressed suit, a collared blouse and one strand of perils to a luncheon with the company CEO.

Product List

PRODUCT	PRICE

Product List

PRODUCT	PRICE

Product List

PRODUCT	PRICE

Product List

PRODUCT	PRICE

New Product

PRODUCT	PRICE

New Product

PRODUCT	PRICE

New Product

PRODUCT	PRICE

New Product

PRODUCT	PRICE

Marketing planner

Marketing planner

Marketing planner

Marketing planner

How You Can Track Your Business Income?

A company's income is directly proportional to the sales of products or the sale of its services. In order to track the income of a company's business, one must have a clear idea regarding the company's expenses. Considering the cash inflows and the calculating the expenses of the company gives us the reports regarding the company's profit or loss. These all things are mutually interconnected with each other in such a way that if the sales are increasing, the company's profit will be increasing and ultimately the income of the company will also increase and vice versa.

As long as the sum of the cash inflow is higher as compared to the expenses of the company, the company will remain in profitable state. And maintaining the profitable state of a company is really important in order to expand the market shares of the company.

STEPS TO BE FOLLOWED:

Following are some of the ways through which we can conveniently tract the business income whether weekly or monthly or even annually according to the needs.

- First of all, a business must have an operational bank account in order to make secure transactions as well as to keep everything on the records.

- Secondly, choose an appropriate accounting system for your business. This can be any software or simply a Microsoft Excel sheet which can be used as a business worksheet to record all the expenses as well as all the incomes. While using this technique, prefer cash accounting as it will be much simpler and everything can be recorded conveniently.

- Try to connect your banking account with your accounting system or software you are using. This will give you access to all the transactions made regarding your business at just one tap.

- Try managing all the receipts. This will surely help out at the end of the week, month or year according to your income tracking routine.

- Record all the expenses promptly. Because all the expenses and the incomes are accountable.

Business Budget And Budget Sheet

A business budget is actually the allocation or allotment of the revenue for specific tasks, jobs, expenditures etc. This will also describe that how much budget to be spent daily, weekly, monthly or annually. A well managed budget always considers each and every expense that includes the needs of the business or the expenses required to run the business.

A personal budget worksheet allows a person or a business to determine the state of their finances and help them plan their expenses over a period of a month or a year. A budget spreadsheet manages money and allocates sufficient amount for each expense without depleting the cash flow. A business budget sheet acts as a backbone for any business or company as without it, no-one will have any idea regarding the expenses or the total revenue left behind and there will be greater chances of mismanagement and also for the company going into the loss state. Mainly, a budget sheet helps us to plan things accordingly.

DETERMINING THE PROFITABILITY:

Through this type of evaluation, any business holder can determine the profitability of the business and can do further calculations that whether the business can afford its expenses as well as expansion. Doing this practice continuously will make a chart of the company's performance and the owner as well as the management can view the performance of the business and can take steps in order to improve the performance if the chart was seen declining.

Expense Tracker

DATE	DESCRIPTION	CATEGORY	AMOUNT

Expense Tracker

DATE	DESCRIPTION	CATEGORY	AMOUNT

Cost Profit Form

PRODUCT	COST	PRICE	PROFIT

Cost Profit Form

PRODUCT	COST	PRICE	PROFIT

Income Tracker

DATE	DESCRIPTION	CATEGORY	AMOUNT

Income Tracker

DATE	DESCRIPTION	CATEGORY	AMOUNT

"Hard work is the mother of good luck."

Sales Tracker

DATE	ITEM	REVENUE	SHIP DATE

Sales Tracker

DATE	ITEM	REVENUE	SHIP DATE

Profit Report

Month

MONTH	SALES INCOME	PRODUCT COSTS	SHIPPING LIST	PROFIT

Profit Report

Month

MONTH	SALES INCOME	PRODUCT COSTS	SHIPPING LIST	PROFIT

How To Generate Leads To Make Money?

In the context of business, one may refer leads as a contact that can prove vital in terms of sales or can act as a potential customer. Leads can prove beneficial or vital for every business but they can result as the backbone of the new startups as well as small businesses.

Leads Generation:

Before moving further, we must have an idea that how we can generate leads or how we can identify the ways in which we can convert contacts into leads. The following steps will prove beneficial in this regard:

- The main and the foremost step in any business is to identify the audience to be targeted, like stores selling children's clothes will try to target mostly the ladies of a specific age group. And their content will be designed accordingly.

- After choosing the audience and content, the next step will be its promotion. Choose the promotional method wisely in order to reach the targeted audience.

- After promotion, the customers will reach the business. It will be the responsibility of the business holder to create a sales funnel.

- Once a customer shops from your business, make a relationship with them by contacting them through email via your weekly or monthly newsletter. Relationship can also be strengthened by using social media platforms.

- Taking customers feedback is one of the main thing that attracts many other customers towards your business. Must value your customers feedback and try to improve on daily basis.

Apart from this, any business holder or anyone can convert their contacts to the leads by using the above mentioned steps in a chronological manner.

Earning Money From Leads:

Once the leads are created, they can prove to be a continuous source of income or sales if and only if the basic three things of the business are effective from the rest of the brands, that are quality, quantity and cost. If any of the things are compromised at the startup time, the business may move towards collapse due to negative feedback and lack of interest of the targeted audience.

Like, if a new business has a higher cost of its products as compared to an existing and customers known brand, hardly any customer will get attention. The cost must be in accordance to the type of customers your business is targeting. The same goes for the quality of the products. If the quality is compromised at any stage, the customers whether they are new or old, may loose the interest in that particular brand. Time, is also an important step for some businesses like e-stores and software houses that are supposed to deliver the products on time.

Don't try to convert those contacts to leads whom you know might not prove beneficial like some people only do things just for the sake of fun and nothing more. So, again, the same thing, target the right audience to get the adequate results.

Contacts

Name:

Phone:

Email:

Address:

Name:

Phone:

Email:

Address:

Name:

Phone:

Email:

Address:

Name:

Phone:

Email:

Address:

Name:

Phone:

Email:

Address:

Name:

Phone:

Email:

Address:

Contacts

Name:

Phone:

Email:

Address:

Name:

Phone:

Email:

Address:

Name:

Phone:

Email:

Address:

Name:

Phone:

Email:

Address:

Name:

Phone:

Email:

Address:

Name:

Phone:

Email:

Address:

Business Contacts

NAME	EMAIL	NUMBER

Business Contacts

NAME	EMAIL	NUMBER

Customer Contacts

NAME	EMAIL	NUMBER

Customer Contacts

NAME	EMAIL	NUMBER

Personal Contacts

NAME	EMAIL	NUMBER

Personal Contacts

NAME	EMAIL	NUMBER

Other Contacts

NAME	EMAIL	NUMBER

Other Contacts

NAME	EMAIL	NUMBER

Email List

NAME	EMAIL ADDRESS

Email List

NAME	EMAIL ADDRESS

Why is it important for self contractors and small business owners to file taxes

The Internal Revenue Service helps citizens about the significance of filing taxes on time and marking goods on their assessments. There are a few choices accessible to help individuals who are experiencing difficulty in paying taxes.

Citizens should document on schedule(i.e., pay at least some amount), regardless of whether they can't pay everything due. After some time, they should spend the rest in a hurry. Keep in mind; the sooner paid, the less owed.

Benefits for filing taxes on time:

- Stay away from added interest and punishments.

- Try not to lose future refunds. Part or the entirety of any value is first used to repay any expenses owed.

- Defend credit if the IRS documents an assessment lien against a citizen; it could influence FICO ratings and make it harder to get a credit.

Self Employed/Contractors and Small Business Owners Tax Obligations

Self-employed contractors, including consultants, should consider their charges when setting their estimating, view their taxation rate in arranging their funds for the year (e.g., setting aside cash versus reinvesting it in the business), and track their operational expense to deduct them toward the year's end.

The IRS orders self-employed people into the accompanying classifications:

- Carrying on an exchange or business as a sole owner or a self-employed entity.

- Being an individual from an organization that carries on an exchange or business.

- Being generally in business for yourself (in simple terms, freelancing or part-time).

As per Pew Research, around 15 million Americans self-employed. In such cases, you should pay an income tax as well as self-employment tax.

If you have a small business, regardless of whether sole ownership, association, LLC, or company, you must make sure to pay self-employment tax and record Schedule SE to Form 1040 if you acquire benefits of $400 or more a given year from the business. You can check out the IRS website for details.

Schedule C

A Schedule C structure is the tax document utilized by a sole owner to figure his business' net benefit or deficit. At that point, this sum will be used on the owner's very own annual assessment form to sort out his absolute duty obligation for the year.

All sole ownerships should record a Schedule C ("Profit or Loss from Business/Sole Proprietorship") with their duties. A Schedule C structure is an itemized structure as figures for money, costs, and merchandise offered, all should be recorded. A net benefit or shortfall figure will at that point be determined and afterward utilized on the owner's very own annual assessment form (on structure 1040).

Minimum Income to file Schedule C

There is no base pay to record Schedule C. All Income and costs should be accounted for on the Schedule C, no matter how less you earned.

There is a base limit of $400 for paying self-employment tax. So, suppose if you are earning up to $400, you will not fall under the obligation to pay tax. In any case, don't get that mistaken for not expecting to report your self-employment income.

Tax Checklist

General

- ☐ _____
- ☐ _____
- ☐ _____
- ☐ _____
- ☐ _____
- ☐ _____

Income

- ☐ _____
- ☐ _____
- ☐ _____
- ☐ _____
- ☐ _____
- ☐ _____

Adjustments/Credit

- ☐ _____
- ☐ _____
- ☐ _____
- ☐ _____
- ☐ _____
- ☐ _____

Paid Taxes

- ☐ _____
- ☐ _____
- ☐ _____
- ☐ _____
- ☐ _____
- ☐ _____

Retirement

- ☐ _____
- ☐ _____
- ☐ _____
- ☐ _____
- ☐ _____
- ☐ _____

Medical

- ☐ _____
- ☐ _____
- ☐ _____
- ☐ _____
- ☐ _____
- ☐ _____

Charitable

- ☐ _____
- ☐ _____
- ☐ _____
- ☐ _____
- ☐ _____
- ☐ _____

Misc./Extras

- ☐ _____
- ☐ _____
- ☐ _____
- ☐ _____
- ☐ _____
- ☐ _____

Tax Checklist

General

- [ ] _____
- [ ] _____
- [ ] _____
- [ ] _____
- [ ] _____
- [ ] _____

Income

- [ ] _____
- [ ] _____
- [ ] _____
- [ ] _____
- [ ] _____
- [ ] _____

Adjustments/Credit

- [ ] _____
- [ ] _____
- [ ] _____
- [ ] _____
- [ ] _____
- [ ] _____

Paid Taxes

- [ ] _____
- [ ] _____
- [ ] _____
- [ ] _____
- [ ] _____
- [ ] _____

Retirement

- [ ] _____
- [ ] _____
- [ ] _____
- [ ] _____
- [ ] _____
- [ ] _____

Medical

- [ ] _____
- [ ] _____
- [ ] _____
- [ ] _____
- [ ] _____
- [ ] _____

Charitable

- [ ] _____
- [ ] _____
- [ ] _____
- [ ] _____
- [ ] _____
- [ ] _____

Misc./Extras

- [ ] _____
- [ ] _____
- [ ] _____
- [ ] _____
- [ ] _____
- [ ] _____

Tax Worksheet

- [ ] _____
- [ ] _____
- [ ] _____
- [ ] _____
- [ ] _____
- [ ] _____
- [ ] _____
- [ ] _____
- [ ] _____
- [ ] _____
- [ ] _____
- [ ] _____

Donations

DATE	ITEM DESCRIPTION	WHERE DONATED	VALUE

Schedule C Worksheet

	$
Name of Business, If any:	
Type of Business (i.e., electronic repair. HR Consulting. etc)	
Employer ID (if applicable)	
Accounting Method:	
Income: Gross receipts:	
Other Income:	
• ANY income at all? If not cash or "rear money, perhaps you had "bartering. income in the form of traded services, etc?	
COST OF GOODS SOLD	
Beginning Inventory	
Purchases	
Cost of Labor	
Material & Supplies	
Ending Inventory	

OTHER EXPENCES

Advertising		Pension and Profit Sharing	
Bad Debt		Rent — Vehicles /Machinery	
Car and Truck.		Rent — Other	
Parking Fees and Tolls		Repairs and Maintenance	
Commissions and Fees			
Employee Benefits		Supplies	
Health Insurance		Business Taxes	
Insurance — Other		Business Licenses & Fees	
Insurance — Mortgage		Utilities	
Interest — Other		Wagm	
Legal and Professional Fees		Other EX,ISCS: list	
Education and Training			

Notes

Notes

Notes

Notes

Notes

Notes

Notes

Notes

Notes

_____

_____

_____

_____

_____

_____

_____

_____

_____

_____

_____

_____

_____

_____

_____

_____

Notes

www.ingramcontent.com/pod-product-compliance
Lightning Source LLC
Chambersburg PA
CBHW081817200326
41597CB00023B/4280